student WORKBOOK

AQA (A)

A2 Psychology
Treating Mental Disorders
Molly Marshall

Introduction	2
Topic 1 Biological (somatic) therapies	3
Topic 2 Behavioural therapies	20
Topic 3 Alternative therapies	36

Philip Allan Updates
Market Place, Deddington, Oxfordshire OX15 0SE

Orders
Bookpoint Ltd, 130 Milton Park, Abingdon, Oxfordshire, OX14 4SB
tel: 01235 827720, fax: 01235 400454
e-mail: uk.orders@bookpoint.co.uk
Lines are open 9.00 a.m.–5.00 p.m., Monday to Saturday, with a 24-hour message answering service. You can also order through the Philip Allan Updates website: www.philipallan.co.uk

© Philip Allan Updates 2007

ISBN 978-1-84489-480-2

All rights reserved; no part of this publication may be reproduced, stored in a retrieval system, or transmitted, in any form or by any means, electronic, mechanical, photocopying, recording or otherwise without either the prior written permission of Philip Allan Updates or a licence permitting restricted copying in the United Kingdom issued by the Copyright Licensing Agency Ltd, 90 Tottenham Court Road, London W1T 4LP.

Printed in Spain

Philip Allan Updates' policy is to use papers that are natural, renewable and recyclable products and made from wood grown in sustainable forests. The logging and manufacturing processes are expected to conform to the environmental regulations of the country of origin.

Introduction

The aim of this workbook is to help you to increase your understanding of the treatment of mental disorders and to improve your skills in answering the types of question you might encounter in the AQA (A) A2 examination.

The workbook includes a variety of stimulus material that will help you to learn about psychological research, terminology and concepts. The questions are wide-ranging and designed to support you as you develop skills of analysis, interpretation and evaluation. Writing answers to the questions will help you learn to communicate your knowledge and understanding of psychology in a clear and effective manner. The questions are organised so that they become progressively more difficult within each topic. As you complete the workbook, you will be learning the content required for the exam and also how to write effective answers that will achieve high marks.

Topic 1 focuses on biological therapies, including chemotherapy, ECT and psychosurgery. Topic 2 covers behavioural therapies, including those based on classical conditioning (e.g. flooding) and those based on operant conditioning (e.g. token economies). Topic 3 focuses on alternatives to biological and behavioural therapies. You need to study therapies derived from either the psychodynamic model of abnormality (e.g. psychoanalysis and psychodrama) or from the cognitive-behavioural model (e.g. rational emotive therapy and stress-inoculation therapy). This workbook focuses on cognitive-behavioural therapies.

In each topic area, the ethical issues surrounding the use of the therapies, such as their appropriateness and effectiveness, are discussed.

To gain maximum benefit, you should complete the topics and questions in the order given. There are several ways in which you can use this workbook:

(1) As an integral part of your learning experience, in conjunction with your class notes, handouts and textbook. Periodically, your teacher might ask you to hand your book in for assessment.

(2) As a revision tool, in which case you should work through the topics, writing the answers as practice for the exam.

(3) As a combination of **(1)** and **(2)** — if, as you progress through the module, you write answers to all the questions in this book, at the end of the course you will have created a valuable resource from which to revise.

Whichever way you choose, I hope the workbook will help you in your studies and in your exam.

Topic 1 Biological (somatic) therapies

People who experience mental disorders need appropriate treatment. Finding an effective treatment can depend on what is perceived to be the cause of the disorder. If a mental disorder is thought to have a biological cause — for example, a chemical imbalance in the brain — then a biological treatment would be offered because these treatments change the body's biological processes. Biological (somatic) treatments include:
- drug therapies (chemotherapy)
- electroconvulsive therapy (ECT)
- psychosurgery (surgical procedures)

In this topic you will learn about a range of biological (somatic) treatments and will consider the ethical issues related to these treatments, as well as the appropriateness and effectiveness of each treatment. The appropriateness of a therapy is judged by its suitability for a particular disorder; the effectiveness of a treatment is judged by how well it works. This is a complex topic, so you should refer to your textbook and the internet to read round the topic and familiarise yourself with the new and sometimes challenging vocabulary.

Item 1
Drug treatments (chemotherapy)

Drug treatments, known as chemotherapy, work by changing the biological processes in the brain or other parts of the body and even the way a person thinks or behaves. Some drugs alter the chemical functioning of the brain by affecting the action of neurotransmitters. A neurotransmitter is a chemical that transmits impulses across the tiny gaps (synapses) between nerve cells. Very small changes in the neurotransmitter systems in the brain lead to changes in moods, feelings, perception and behaviour.

Drugs affect neurotransmitters in several different ways. Some drugs are similar to a specific neurotransmitter, which they 'imitate'. They interfere with the activity of the neurotransmitter by moving into its receptor sites. Some drugs, such as the **antipsychotic** drugs used to treat schizophrenia, block receptor sites so that the effects of a neurotransmitter are reduced. Other drugs, such as the **antidepressant** selective serotonin reuptake inhibitors (SSRIs), slow down the reuptake of the neurotransmitter(s) so they remain in the synapses for longer.

Item 2
Drugs and their side effects

Antipsychotic drugs (neuroleptics)

Chlorpromazine and clozapine are antipsychotic drugs used to treat schizophrenia. They work by reducing the effect of the neurotransmitter dopamine. This results in a reduction in psychotic symptoms such as delusions and hallucinations. The side effects of antipsychotics can be minor, for example tiredness or sleepiness. However, long-term medication with drugs such as chlorpromazine and clozapine can lead to a shuffling gait, slow speech and even involuntary spasms of the face (tardive dyskinesia).

Antidepressants

Two types of antidepressant drug are tricyclics and SSRIs (e.g. Prozac). They are used to treat depression, phobias and obsessive–compulsive disorder. Depression is thought to be the result of having too little of the neurotransmitters serotonin and norepinephrine. Tricyclic drugs work by blocking the mechanism that reabsorbs these neurotransmitters. This results in more of these neurotransmitter substances remaining in the synapses. Side effects of tricyclic drugs include blurred vision, dry mouth, weight gain and constipation. SSRIs block the reuptake of the neurotransmitter serotonin. Side effects of SSRIs such as Prozac include digestive problems, headaches, insomnia, aggressiveness and even suicidal thoughts.

Antianxiety (anxiolytic) drugs

Valium is an example of a drug used to reduce the symptoms of anxiety disorders. It is a member of the benzodiazepine family. Benzodiazepine drugs work by increasing the action of gamma-aminobutyric acid (GABA), a substance that slows down the transmission of signals in the brain. Some side effects of benzodiazepine drugs are serious and it is dangerous to mix them with alcohol and some other medicines. Also, long-term use can lead to dependence. This means that withdrawal symptoms may be experienced if patients stop taking this type of drug suddenly.

Methylphenidate (Ritalin)

Methylphenidate (Ritalin) is a medication, in pill form, prescribed for individuals (usually children) who are abnormally active or who suffer from 'attention-deficit hyperactivity disorder' (ADHD). Ritalin is a central nervous system stimulant, which works by increasing dopamine levels in the brain, paradoxically having a calming effect on hyperactive children and a focusing effect on those with attention deficit.

Item 3
Drugs: effectiveness and appropriateness

Antipsychotic drugs

These drugs allow disturbed psychotic patients to live outside a psychiatric hospital because they reduce the positive symptoms of the disorder, such as delusions, hallucinations and disordered thoughts. However, chlorpromazine does not change the negative symptoms of schizophrenia, for example lack of motivation and social withdrawal.

Gelder et al. (1999) reported that clozapine is effective in those patients who do not respond to the more traditional drug, chlorpromazine. Clozapine may also treat the negative symptoms of schizophrenia and it causes fewer serious side effects.

The World Health Organization **(WHO 2001)** reported that relapse rates in schizophrenics after 1 year of treatment were 55% with a placebo, 25% with chlorpromazine and between 2% and 23% when chlorpromazine was combined with family therapy. This suggests that the antipsychotic drug was an effective treatment.

Antidepressants

The World Health Organization **(WHO 2001)** concluded that SSRIs are as effective as tricyclic drugs in the treatment of severe depression and that they have fewer unwanted side effects. **Costello et al. (1995)** reported that Prozac (an SSRI) is the most commonly prescribed antidepressant, having been taken by more than 38 million people since its launch in 1988.

Fisher and Greenberg (1995) looked at 15 literature reviews and conducted two large-scale meta-analyses of the use of antidepressants. They reported a relapse rate greater than 60% among people who had responded positively to the drugs and who later ceased to take them. This suggests that the drugs are effective.

Moncrieff and Cohen (2005) proposed an alternative explanation for the effectiveness of antidepressants. They suggested that they may work by causing sedation, which reduces the agitation associated with depression, induces sleep and masks depressive feelings. Antidepressants may also work by enhancing the placebo effect, because physiological reactions to a drug confirm to patients that they are taking an active medication — in which case almost anything that causes a physiological reaction might be found to have antidepressant properties.

Concerns have been raised about the appropriateness of SSRIs. In some people, Prozac is known to cause an agitated state of mind and an urge to commit murder or suicide. According to **Boseley (1999)**, approximately 250,000 people have attempted suicide because of the drug and about 25,000 may have succeeded. In the USA in 1998, after having taken the SSRI Paxil for only 2 days, Donald Schell, aged 60, murdered his wife, daughter and granddaughter and then committed suicide. His remaining family successfully sued the drug manufacturers.

However, **Khan et al. (2000)** reviewed the data from 45 clinical trials in which patients were assigned either to treatment by antidepressant drugs or to placebo-comparison conditions. The findings were that:
- in cases of suicide or attempted suicide there was no significant difference between treatment and placebo groups
- there was a positive correlation between the length of the trial and symptom reduction
- the placebo groups reported symptom reduction — though to a lesser extent than the active treatment groups

Taken together, these findings tend to suggest not only that antidepressant drugs do not increase suicidal thoughts but also that they are not very effective.

Antianxiety (anxiolytic) drugs

Anxiolytic drugs are widely prescribed in the UK. In 1989, there were 21 million prescriptions for Librium and Valium. They are used to treat severe anxiety and should only be prescribed for a short period (2–3 weeks). **Dubvosky (1990)** reported that 35% of patients with generalised anxiety disorder benefited from taking benzodiazepines and another 40% gained moderate relief. However, only short-term treatment is appropriate because if the drugs are taken for more than 6 months, dependency may develop. The effects of withdrawal include anxiety and muscle tremors.

The 'hello–goodbye effect'

It has been suggested that patients may overstate their symptoms at the start of treatment in order to ensure care, and understate their symptoms at the end of treatment to show gratitude. This 'hello–goodbye' effect would tend to make drug treatment (or any treatment) appear more effective.

Item 4
Drugs: appropriateness and limitations

Appropriateness
- Most drug treatments are effective in relieving symptoms for many people, enabling them to manage day-to-day life more easily.
- Drug treatment only requires that patients remember to take the drugs and does not require them to make either much effort or lifestyle changes.
- Drug treatments can be used to relieve symptoms in order to help the patient prepare for another type of therapy, or can be used alongside another therapy.

Limitations
- Drug treatments do not work for everybody. Individuals can respond differently to the same drug treatments and drug-induced side effects can be a problem.
- Unless there is a clearly understood biological cause for the problem, drugs are unlikely to provide a long-term cure. Also, drugs may only provide temporary relief from symptoms. When the patient stops taking the drugs, the symptoms may return.
- **Brown (2003)** reported that of studies reporting significant findings, 81% were published; of studies reporting non-significant findings, 68% were published. This bias in publication may lead drug treatments to be perceived to be more effective than they really are.

Item 5
Electroconvulsive therapy (ECT) and psychosurgery

ECT is a treatment in which a brief electrical stimulus is given to the brain via electrodes placed on the temples. The electrical charge lasts 1–4 seconds and causes an epileptic-like seizure. Before treatment, the patient is anaesthetised and given an injection of muscle relaxant that depresses the breathing, and oxygen is given until the patient is able to breathe naturally again. The ECT electrodes can be placed on both sides of the head (bilateral placement) or on one side of the head (unilateral placement). Unilateral placement is usually to the non-dominant side of the brain, with the aim of reducing cognitive side effects. The current needed to induce a seizure (the seizure threshold) can vary up to 40-fold between individuals. Most patients receive a total of six to twelve ECT treatments at a rate of one a day, three times a week.

ECT is usually given to people with severe depression who have not responded to other forms of treatment, such as antidepressant drugs. However, it is sometimes used to treat people diagnosed with bipolar affective disorder (manic depression) or schizophrenia. It is usually given only after the risks have been explained and with the patient's consent. Under certain strict conditions, and according to current UK legislation, ECT can be given without the patient's consent.

Side effects of ECT can include fear and anxiety, retrograde amnesia and headaches. **Rose et al. (2003)** suggested that 33% of patients report long-term memory loss.

There are several theories about how ECT works:
- **Neurotransmitter theory** — ECT works like antidepressant medication, changing the way brain receptors receive important mood-related chemicals.
- **Anticonvulsant theory** — ECT-induced seizures teach the brain to resist seizures. This effort to inhibit seizures dampens abnormally active brain circuits, stabilising mood.
- **Neuroendocrine theory** — the seizure causes the hypothalamus to release chemicals that regulate mood.
- **Brain damage theory** — shock damages the brain, causing memory loss and disorientation. This creates a temporary illusion that 'problems' are gone.
- **Psychological theory** — depressed people often feel guilty, and ECT satisfies their need for punishment. Alternatively, the dramatic nature of ECT and the nursing care afterwards make patients feel that they are being taken seriously, i.e. the placebo effect.

Item 6
Is ECT an effective and appropriate treatment?

Corner (2002) states that 60–70% of patients improve following ECT treatment, but that the effects may not last.
Sackheim et al. (2001) found that 84% of patients relapsed within 6 months of ECT treatment.

Guidance on the use of ECT
Although ECT has been used since the 1930s, there is still no generally accepted theory that explains its mechanism of action. The most prevalent hypothesis is that it causes an alteration in the post-synaptic response to central nervous system neurotransmitters. ECT administration affects the central nervous system and causes changes in cardiovascular dynamics. The mortality associated with ECT is reported not to be in excess of that associated with the administration of a general anaesthetic for minor surgery.

The evidence suggests that the short-term effectiveness of ECT in individuals with severe depressive illness has been demonstrated. However, there is less evidence to suggest that ECT is effective in the acute treatment of catatonia and mania (symptoms of acute schizophrenia). The evidence for the effectiveness of ECT in schizophrenia in general was not conclusive and, therefore, ECT is not recommended for this population.

There was no conclusive evidence to support the effectiveness of ECT beyond the short term or to suggest that it is more beneficial as a maintenance therapy in depressive illness than drug treatments currently available. There is concern that the value of electroconvulsive maintenance therapy remains unproven in the context of the lack of information on whether the adverse effects of ECT (for example, on cognitive function) may be cumulative with repeated administration.

Although ECT may be an effective treatment for certain subgroups of people with mental disorders, opinion in patients varies from those who consider that its adverse effects are tolerable to those who consider that it is associated with unacceptable side effects. While some individuals considered ECT to be a beneficial treatment, others reported feelings of terror, shame and distress, and found it harmful and an abusive invasion of personal autonomy, especially when it was administered without their consent. NICE concluded that it is essential to obtain valid and informed consent by following recognised guidelines, and that consent should never be obtained by coercion through threat of compulsory treatment under the Mental Health Act.

Source: Main points taken from the National Institute for Clinical Excellence (NICE) (2003): www.nice.org.uk

Item 7
Psychosurgery: historical perspective

Psychosurgery means brain surgery as a treatment for mental disorders. In 1936, Moniz and Lima treated 20 patients with severe anxiety, obsessional behaviour and irrational fears. They severed fibres connecting subcortical areas of the brain with the frontal lobes. The operation was called 'prefrontal leucotomy'. Approximately a third of these patients were alleged to have improved, a third to have worsened and a third were unchanged. Moniz was the first person to use the term 'psychosurgery'. In 1949, he won the Nobel Prize for Medicine for development of the prefrontal leucotomy. (Unfortunately, he was later paralysed when he was shot by one of his former 'lobotomised' patients!)

In 1936, a neurologist, Walter Freeman, and a neurosurgeon, James Watts, began to treat patients with depression by using an operation they termed 'bilateral frontal leucotomy'. This procedure became known as the 'Freeman–Watts lobotomy'. In 1945, Freeman developed the transorbital leucotomy. This procedure, also known as the 'ice-pick lobotomy', involved inserting an instrument under the eyelids, through the roof of the eye orbit into the frontal cortex of the brain, where a sweeping motion cut the cortical tissue. In the UK between 1942 and 1952, 10,000 of these operations were performed, 66% of which were on people diagnosed with schizophrenia.

In the USA in 1947, Spiegel, a neurologist, and Wycis, a neurosurgeon, performed the first stereotactic neurosurgical operation in a patient with a psychiatric disorder. The development of stereotaxis (small amounts of brain tissue are destroyed in precise locations) allowed much greater accuracy when causing lesions in specific brain areas.

Item 8
Psychosurgery in the UK

A variety of stereotactic techniques are in use at different treatment centres, all of which are irreversible. The techniques are called 'stereotactic' because they involve the use of specially constructed frames that are attached to the patient's skull and hold the probes that are put into the brain. Used together with neuroimaging (computerised tomography (CT) or magnetic resonance imaging (MRI) scans) and dedicated computer software, stereotactic techniques allow the probes to be guided precisely — to within 1 mm of any desired target within the brain. The stereotactic frame means that the siting of the probe is fixed and mechanical, so there is no error due to faltering hand movements. The procedure is carried out under general anaesthetic and lasts approximately 90 minutes, most of this time being taken up with X-rays to monitor the position of the probe.

The Mental Health Act Commission panel authorised seven psychosurgery operations to go ahead in England and Wales in 1999–2000 and two in 2000–01. Prior to that, records show:
1997–99 — 17 such operations in England and Wales
1993 — 23 such operations in England, Scotland and Wales
1992 — 27 such operations in England and Scotland
1991 — 17 such operations in England
1990 — 26 such operations in England

Item 9
Is psychosurgery an effective and appropriate treatment?

Effectiveness
The following statistics suggest that psychosurgery can be an effective treatment

Table 1 Outcomes by surgical technique

Operation	Overall success rate (%)	Success rate for major affective disorder (%)	Success rate for OCD (%)
Anterior capsulotomy	67	55	45
Anterior cingulotomy	61	65	56
Subcaudate tractotomy	37	34	33

Source: MIND (1996) CGI — I *(Clinical Global Impression of Change — Improvement), meta-analysis of psychosurgery outcomes*

Table 2 Combined outcomes by diagnosis

Effect	Depression (n = 727)	OCD (n = 478)	Anxiety disorder (n = 290)
Marked improvement	63%	58%	52%
Lesser improvement	22%	27%	25%
No response	14%	14%	21%
Worse	1%	1%	2%

Source: MIND (1996) CGI — I *(Clinical Global Impression of Change — Improvement), meta-analysis of psychosurgery outcomes*

Side effects of psychosurgery

Some of the side effects, such as damage to blood vessels, confused states and epilepsy, can be associated with any brain operation. Other adverse effects include headaches, which may be severe and, in the long term, weight gain and apathy. Weight gain is associated with the anterior capsulotomy and subcaudate tractotomy procedures, but not with anterior cingulotomy. A degree of personality change has been reported in some people, but this is considered to be rare. There is no evidence that psychosurgery causes intellectual impairment. Indeed, in some cases IQ scores have improved. This is probably because of the relief of symptoms that had severely impaired concentration before treatment. Psychiatrists have said that if the risk of suicide is reduced and some lives are saved, then that is enough to justify the treatment.

Statement by MIND

MIND is the leading mental health charity in the UK. It has made the following statement:

> Psychosurgery is used where no other treatments have helped, in particular for severe obsessive–compulsive problems or depression. Though these techniques are more precise than in the past, psychosurgery involves the destruction of brain tissue or function, is irreversible and carries a risk of apathy, excessive weight gain, loss of inhibition and epilepsy. Although follow-up studies show the majority of patients seem to improve, these uncontrolled studies have been said to provide 'virtually no scientific support for the efficacy of the treatment at all'. The research has been criticised for failing to assess adverse effects adequately, especially the effect on personality; neither does it adequately assess users' views of outcome.

MIND is concerned that failure to relieve suffering may lead towards increasingly invasive procedures, and is particularly concerned about the use of irreversible procedures that carry serious risks when so little is known about their action. MIND is not happy with the continued use of psychosurgery and believes that there should be a rigorous review to determine whether continued use is justified.

Item 10
Ethical issues arising from biological treatments

Ethical issues include:
- **All treatments** — can people who are mentally disturbed make the decision as to the type of treatment they will have?
- **Chemotherapy** — to what extent can people ever give fully informed consent if they do not know what the side effects of drug treatment may be?
- **ECT** — if we do not know 'how and why' ECT works, to what extent can it be ethical to recommend it as a treatment?
- **Psychosurgery** — if the outcome of psychosurgery is uncertain and irreversible, to what extent can it ever be ethical to recommend it as a treatment?

1 Read your textbook and Items 1–8.
  a Fill in the blanks to complete the sentences.

  b Explain why a biological treatment may be proposed for a psychological disorder.

Answers

1a (i) Drugs used to treat schizophrenia are called ....

   (ii) Conventional antipsychotic drugs increase the level of the neurotransmitter ....

   (iii) SSRI drugs increase the level of the neurotransmitter ....

   (iv) ECT stands for ....

   (v) ECT is usually given to people with severe .... who have not responded to other treatment.

   (vi) Surgery that takes place when specially constructed frames are attached to a patient's skull to hold the probes that are inserted into the brain is called ....

   (vii) .... has proposed that uncontrolled trials provide virtually no scientific support for the efficacy of ECT.

   (viii) The SSRI .... is the most commonly prescribed antidepressant.

   (ix) Valium is used to treat severe .... and should only be prescribed for a .... period.

   (x) The mechanism that reabsorbs the neurotransmitters serotonin and norepinephrine is blocked by .... antidepressants.

 b ....

....

....

....

AQA (A) A2 Psychology: Treating Mental Disorders **11**

A2 Psychology: Treating Mental Disorders

Topic 1 Biological (somatic) therapies

c Explain how drug treatments affect the brain and, therefore, behaviour.

c ....
....
....
....
....

d Complete the table by stating whether the statements are true or false.

d

Statement	True/False
Clozapine is an antipsychotic drug	
Neuroleptic drugs reduce the positive symptoms of schizophrenia	
Dopamine is a neurotransmitter	
Some antidepressant drugs are tricyclics	
Prozac is a tricyclic drug	
SSRI drugs block the reuptake of the neurotransmitter serotonin	
Depression may result from too little serotonin	
Anxiolytic drugs make you anxious	
Valium can be used to reduce the symptoms of anxiety disorders	
Anxiolytics such as Valium are benzodiazepines	
Benzodiazepine drugs are addictive	
It is safe to drink alcohol while taking benzodiazepines	

e When is a drug treatment judged to be effective?

f When is a drug treatment judged to be appropriate?

2 Read your textbook and Items 1–4. Complete each of the following paragraphs (by quoting evidence) to write an evaluative commentary on the use of drugs in the treatment of mental disorders.
  a Gelder et al. (1999) reported that clozapine is effective in those patients who do not respond to the more traditional drug, chlorpromazine. It may also treat the negative symptoms of schizophrenia and it causes fewer serious side effects.

e

f

2a However…

A2 Psychology: Treating Mental Disorders

Topic 1 Biological (somatic) therapies

b Costello et al. (1995) reported that the SSRI Prozac is the most commonly prescribed antidepressant, having been taken by more than 38 million people since its launch in 1988.

b However…

c Fisher and Greenberg (1995) examined 15 literature reviews and conducted two large-scale meta-analyses of the use of antidepressants. They reported a relapse rate greater than 60% among people who had responded positively to the drugs and who later ceased to take them.

c However…

d Dubvosky (1990) reported that 35% of patients with generalised anxiety disorder benefit from taking benzodiazepines and another 40% gain moderate relief.

d However…

3 Read your textbook and Items 5 and 6. Petronella is a patient in a psychiatric hospital who has been severely depressed for many months. She has been taking antidepressants but they have not helped her. Her psychiatrist has now suggested that she might be helped by a course of ECT treatment.
a Outline what happens during ECT treatment.

3a

A2 Psychology: Treating Mental Disorders

Topic 1 Biological (somatic) therapies

b Indicate two side effects of ECT treatment that Petronella should be made aware of.

c Before she gives her informed consent, Petronella wants to know how ECT works. Give two hypotheses that suggest how ECT works.

d Petronella has read the NICE report on the use of ECT. As a result, she has decided not to consent to the treatment. Referring to the NICE report, give three reasons why Petronella might refuse ECT treatment.

4 Read your textbook and Items 7–9.
   a Define the term psychosurgery.

   b Who carried out the first psychosurgery, and which mental health problems were they attempting to 'cure'?

   c Outline the surgical procedure called an 'ice-pick lobotomy'.

   d Why was the development of stereotactic psychosurgery advantageous?

4a

b

c

d

A2 Psychology: Treating Mental Disorders

Topic 1 Biological (somatic) therapies

5 Read your textbook and Item 9.

a Using data from Item 9, complete the table.

5a

Statement	True/False
Anterior capsulotomy benefited the majority of patients who suffer OCD	
Anterior cingulotomy benefited the majority of patients with major affective disorder	
The most effective surgical procedure was anterior capsulotomy	

b Use data from Table 2 to answer the following questions:
  (i) What is the total number of patients referred to in the table?
  (ii) Which mental health problem was most improved by psychosurgery? Explain your answer.
  (iii) Which mental health problem was least improved by psychosurgery? Explain your answer.

b (i)

(ii)

(iii)

c Describe some of the side effects of psychosurgery.

c

d Summarise the MIND conclusion about the appropriateness of psychosurgery.

6 Read your textbook and Items 1–10.

> **Exam practice**
>
> *All biological treatments change how the brain and/or body functions, and all treatments have side effects. On a separate piece of paper, answer the following AO2-only questions. You should write about 300 words in answer to each question.*
>
> **a** Chemotherapy has been shown to be an effective treatment for some mental disorders. It can allow people to live 'almost normal' lives. However, all drugs have side effects, which can vary from person to person. To what extent is drug treatment an effective and appropriate way to treat mental disorders?
>
> **b** ECT appears to be effective for some people who suffer from depressive illness. To what extent is ECT an effective and appropriate treatment?

d

6 *Use this space for your planning or notes.*

Topic 2 Behavioural therapies

Not all psychologists agree with physiological explanations for mental disorders. Many propose treatments for mental disorders based on the theory that maladaptive behaviour is learned in the same way as 'normal' behaviour. Replacing maladaptive behaviour with adaptive or desirable behaviour is the aim of behavioural therapies. Behavioural treatments may be based on classical conditioning (e.g. systematic desensitisation) or on operant conditioning (e.g. token economies).

There are important differences between behavioural therapy based on classical or operant conditioning:
- Therapy based on classical conditioning usually aims to remove unwanted behaviour; whereas therapy based on operant conditioning usually aims to develop desirable behaviour.
- Therapy based on classical conditioning involves a reflex behaviour; whereas therapy based on operant conditioning involves behaviour that can be 'chosen'.
- In therapy based on classical conditioning the stimulus for behaviour occurs before the response; whereas in operant conditioning the consequence of behaviour is the stimulus for future behaviour.

This topic covers how such behavioural therapies are used. It considers the ethical issues related to these treatments, as well as the appropriateness and effectiveness of each treatment.

Item 1
Behavioural therapy based on classical conditioning

Behavioural therapies based on classical conditioning assume that some abnormal behaviour is learned. Such behaviour arises because we become conditioned to respond to a particular stimulus (e.g. an object or person) in our environment. Therapies based on classical conditioning usually try to remove undesirable behaviour.

Pavlov's theory of classical conditioning (1927)
Stage 1 Prior to classical conditioning: food (UCS) leads to salivation (UCR).
Stage 2 During classical conditioning: bell (CS) plus food (UCS) leads to salivation (UCR).
Stage 3 After classical conditioning: bell (CS) leads to salivation (CR).

The abbreviations stand for the following:
- **UCS** — unconditioned stimulus
- **UCR** — unconditioned ('normal') reflex response
- **CS** — conditioned stimulus
- **CR** — conditioned reflex response

Extinction happens when the CR no longer occurs — in this case, salivating to the sound of a bell alone. To resurrect the CR, the association of the CS and UCS is required again.

Aversion therapy

Aversion therapy aims to replace a pleasant stimulus–response association with an unpleasant association. It is useful in teaching people to avoid things that are harmful to them. Individuals are repeatedly presented with an unpleasant stimulus (e.g. a drug that makes them feel sick) at the same time as they 'act' the unwanted behaviour (e.g. drink alcohol). The unpleasant stimulus (the drug) acts as the UCS that produces the UCR (e.g. feeling sick). Repeatedly associating the unpleasant stimulus with the undesirable behaviour eventually leads to the situation where drinking alcohol (now the CS) leads to the the CR of feeling sick and, therefore, to the avoidance of alcohol. **Meyer and Chesser (1970)** found that approximately 50% of their alcoholic patients abstained from alcohol for about 1 year following aversion therapy, and that aversion therapy was better than no treatment at all.

Systematic desensitisation

Systematic desensitisation is a type of behavioural therapy in which the undesired behaviour (e.g. a phobia) is broken down into small stimulus–response units. It comprises:
- the construction of a hierarchy of fears
- training in relaxation — the relaxed state is incompatible with anxiety
- graded exposure (in imagination) and relaxation
- homework — practice in real life

For example, in a phobia of snakes, the least stressful situation might be to look at a picture of a snake and the most stressful might be to touch a snake. The therapist works through each stimulus–response unit in the ascending hierarchy, helping the person to replace each dysfunctional response of being afraid with the response of feeling relaxed.

McGrath et al. (1990) reported that 75% of phobic patients responded to systematic desensitisation. Following systematic desensitisation, the majority of patients show improvement in symptoms, but few patients become completely free of anxiety.

Williams and Hargreaves (1995) suggested that neither relaxation nor the construction of a hierarchy is necessary. They reported that all that is required is exposure to the feared stimulus and that the outcome is improved if the feared stimulus is real rather than imaginary. Patients should be exposed to the stimulus until the anxiety has subsided completely, otherwise the exposure may be detrimental.

Flooding

Exposing patients to the real object of their fears until the fear subsides is called flooding. There is evidence to suggest that this is effective.

Wolpe (1973) forced an adolescent girl who had a phobia of cars into the back of a car and drove her round for 4 hours. Although her fear reached hysterical levels, by the end of the journey her fear had disappeared. **Marks (1981)** used flooding as a treatment for agoraphobia (fear of public places) and found this was effective.

Table 1 Therapies based on classical conditioning

Therapy	What happens?	Disorders treated	Effectiveness and ethical issues
Flooding	Exposure to the most feared situation until fear subsides	Some types of specific phobia (e.g. fear of heights)	Successful for many phobias May cause distress
Systematic desensitisation	Gradual exposure to feared situation or object while relaxed	Specific phobias and anxieties (e.g. fear of snakes or of flying)	Effective for many phobias Allows informed consent to be gained Questionable whether person being treated can stop treatment (withdraw) without negative effect
Aversion therapy	Unwanted behaviour is associated with unpleasant stimulus (e.g. feeling sick or electric shock)	Addictive behaviours such as smoking and alcoholism	Unethical because deliberate pain and discomfort inflicted Used in the past to try to change the sexuality of homosexuals, which raises the ethical question of who should judge which behaviours are inappropriate and should be changed

Item 2
Behavioural therapy based on operant conditioning

In behavioural therapies based on operant conditioning (Skinner's theory), the assumption is that behaviour that brings about pleasurable consequences is likely to be repeated. Such therapies are called behaviour modification. Behaviour modification therapies can involve either positive or negative reinforcement:

- **Positive reinforcement** means that the desired behaviour is rewarded by a pleasant consequence. Use of a reward encourages the likelihood of the behaviour being repeated — for example, praising someone for good work encourages (reinforces) its repetition.

- **Negative reinforcement** means that desired behaviour is learned because the consequence of the behaviour is that 'something unpleasant' stops happening (or the person escapes from an aversive stimulus), so pleasure is felt.

Behaviour modification usually involves schedules of reinforcement. Clinical and educational psychologists use behaviour-modification programmes to modify the behaviour of children (or adults) who display challenging behaviour. The ABC model is used to explain how behaviour-modification programmes work:

- **A** — the **antecedent**, i.e. the trigger (stimulus or event) that elicits the behaviour
- **B** — the **behaviour**
- **C** — the **consequence** of the behaviour

Behaviour can be modified by changing either the antecedent or the consequence.

Lovaas et al. (1967) first used operant conditioning with autistic children who had little or no normal speech. The technique they used is called applied behaviour analysis (ABA) and involves a 'behaviour shaping' method. First, verbal approval is paired with a piece of food (positive reinforcement) whenever the child makes eye contact or pays attention to the therapist's voice. Then the child is reinforced with food or praise whenever any kind of speech sound is made. Once speech sounds occur without prompting, the therapist withholds rewards until the child successfully imitates/utters particular letters, then words and finally combinations of words. Many reinforcements are needed before the child imitates simple phrases. **Harris and Handelman (1994)** reviewed the effectiveness of ABA programmes and found that 50% of autistic children who had participated in such programmes were successfully integrated into classes with 'normal' children.

Item 3
Token economy

A **token economy** is a behaviour modification technique sometimes used in psychiatric hospitals, prisons and schools. It involves the use of rewards (reinforcement) for desired behaviours that can be exchanged by the recipient for goods or services.

Neumark (1998) reported a token economy programme used at Wells Park, a residential school for children aged between 7 and 11 years with severe emotional or behavioural difficulties. The token economy system was introduced in 1990 and has been continually refined. Every 5 weeks children, their families and teachers meet to decide and agree the children's 'targets'. Targets might be to 'keep still while I am talking', 'to use a quiet voice' or to 'write in smaller handwriting'. Every 15 minutes each day from Monday to Friday each child has an opportunity to receive a token. Every day at 3.45 p.m. the children can 'cash in' groups of five tokens ('giants') for treats such as books, toys or extra play. More ambitious children can save up 'giants' for shopping trips or outings. The token economy is effective because all the teachers operate the system in the same way. Children previously described as unteachable or hyperactive sit down, read and enjoy learning. In their first year at the school, the reading age of children can increase by 2 or 3 years.

LePage (1999) reported that when a token economy programme was used with patients in a psychiatric unit there was a 43% reduction in the number of violent incidents.

Item 4
Effectiveness of behavioural therapy

Paul and Lentz (1977) compared the effectiveness of three types of therapy. Eighty-four chronic (long-term) and hospitalised psychiatric patients were randomly assigned to one of the three treatment conditions — token economy, milieu therapy and custodial care. Patients were matched for age, gender, socioeconomic status, symptoms and length of hospitalisation. The study had a longitudinal design and lasted 4 years, with an 18-month follow up.

Patients were assessed at 6-monthly intervals, using structured interviews and observations.
- **Token economy therapy.** Acceptable behaviour was modelled and instructed. It was rewarded by tokens that bought necessities, such as meals. Tokens could be saved up to rent better sleeping quarters (e.g. single rooms), to obtain passes to leave the hospital and for luxuries such as staying up later.
- **Milieu therapy.** The hospital became a 'therapeutic community'. Patients were treated as adults who were expected to play a responsible role in the community, in decision making and in their own readjustment. Group (community) interaction was encouraged and staff praised patients who 'did well'.
- **Custodial care.** Patients in the hospital were treated with drugs and were alone 95% of the time. Only short periods of occupational therapy, group therapy and recreation were provided.

The findings were:
- More than 10% of patients in the token economy and milieu therapy groups were able to leave the hospital. The token economy patients were more successful at remaining in the community. No patients in the custodial care group were released.
- The number of patients remaining on antipsychotic drugs was reduced in the token economy and the milieu therapy groups.
- Token economy was the most successful at increasing interpersonal and communication skills.
- Both token economy and milieu therapies reduced symptoms such as delusions, hallucinations and hostile behaviour.

It was concluded that behavioural treatments can help reverse the effects of institutionalisation and can foster the development of social skills.

Item 5
The ethics, effectiveness and appropriateness of behavioural therapy based on operant conditioning

Behaviour modification
- Behavioural modification is effective when rewards rather than punishments are used. However, long-term effectiveness may depend on the reinforcement schedule.
- It may not be appropriate treatment because unpleasant consequences may merely suppress undesirable behaviour, rather than eradicating it.
- When unpleasant consequences are used, it may be unethical.
- It may not be appropriate because treatment deals with symptoms rather than with underlying causes.

Token economy
- A token economy is effective in socialising patients.
- However, it may not be appropriate outside institutions such as schools and hospitals, when rewards are stopped or the context is changed.
- There is an ethical issue regarding the question of who decides which behaviours are 'desired'.

It is important to remember that even when undesirable behaviour is modified, as in the Lovaas ABA programme, the underlying cause of the behaviour remains unchanged. The change in behaviour may help the individual lead a more 'normal' life. However, a different treatment may be more appropriate, depending on the underlying cause. For example, **Jenson (1999)** reported that children with attention-deficit hyperactivity disorder improved more when treated with the drug Ritalin than from participating in behaviour modification programmes.

A2 Psychology: Treating Mental Disorders

1 Read your textbook and Items 1 and 2.
a Fill in the blanks to complete the sentences.

Topic 2 Behavioural therapies

1a (i) Therapies based on the ………………………… approach assume that abnormal behaviour is learned.

(ii) Therapy based on ………………………… ………………………… usually aims to remove unwanted behaviour.

(iii) Therapy based on ………………………… conditioning usually aims to develop ………………………… behaviour.

(iv) ………………………… therapy aims to replace a pleasant stimulus–response association with an unpleasant association.

(v) During ………………………… ………………………… the undesired behaviour (e.g. a phobia) is broken down into small stimulus–response units.

(vi) McGrath et al. (1990) reported that 75% of phobic patients responded to ………………………… ………………………….

(vii) Exposing patients to the real object of their fears until the fear subsides is called …………………………

(viii) In ………………………… ………………………… the desired behaviour is rewarded by a pleasant consequence because the use of a reward encourages the likelihood of the behaviour being repeated.

(ix) In the ABC model, A is the ………………………… (the trigger for the behaviour), B is the ………………………… and C is the ………………………… of the behaviour.

(x) Lovaas et al. (1967) used a technique called ………………………… ………………………… with children who had little or no normal speech.

b Outline the aim of behavioural therapies.

c Outline the process by which abnormal behaviour is learned during classical conditioning.

d Outline how aversion therapy works.

Answers

b

c

d

A2 Psychology: Treating Mental Disorders

Topic 2 Behavioural therapies

e Milton bites his nails until his fingers are very sore. He has tried repeatedly to stop, but has not succeeded. In terms of a treatment based on classical conditioning, suggest how Milton could be helped to stop biting his nails.

f Outline how systematic desensitisation works.

2 Read your textbook and Item 1.

a Sharon is 20 years old and has a phobia of dogs. She has just become engaged to Joe, whose parents have two labradors, so Sharon knows that she must try to cure her phobia. In terms of a treatment based on classical conditioning, suggest how Sharon's dog phobia might be cured.

b Freddie is 6 years old and is afraid of cars. He is so phobic that his mother has to walk 2 miles with him to school every day. Which psychologist used behavioural treatment to cure a car phobia, and how?

A2 Psychology: Treating Mental Disorders

Topic 2 Behavioural therapies

c Describe psychological evidence indicating that behavioural therapies based on classical conditioning are effective.

d Suggest two reasons why treatments based on classical conditioning may give rise to ethical problems.

3 Read your textbook and Items 2, 3 and 4.

a Outline how behaviour modification treatments (based on operant conditioning) work.

b Minerva needs treatment because, although she talks at home, she refuses to speak at all in school. The educational psychologist has been asked to devise a programme to change this 'elective mutism' (people who choose not to speak are called elective mutes). Based on psychological evidence, what therapy would you recommend, and why?

3a

b

Topic 2 Behavioural therapies

c What is a token economy?

d Outline evidence indicating that treatment based on a token economy can be effective.

e Suggest two reasons why the effects of treatments based on operant conditioning may be only short-term.

4 Read your textbook and Items 1–5.

a Outline two differences between therapy based on classical conditioning and therapy based on operant conditioning.

4a

b Suggest why it may be unethical to randomly allocate patients to treatment conditions.

b

A2 Psychology: Treating Mental Disorders

Topic 2 Behavioural therapies

c Treatments based on behavioural approaches may not represent a 'real cure'. To what extent do you agree with this statement, and why?

c

d Continue the sentences in order to complete each 'argument'.

d (i) Behaviour modification by means of a token economy may be unethical because…

5 Read your textbook and all the items in Topics 1 and 2.

Exam practice

On a separate sheet of paper, plan what you will write for the following essay and then write the essay in about 700 words. In the exam you will have about 40 minutes to answer an essay question. Ask your teacher to assess your essay.
Discuss behavioural therapies for mental disorders (e.g. effectiveness and appropriateness).

(ii) Behaviour modification programmes based on operant conditioning may be more ethical than those based on classical conditioning because…

(iii) Behavioural treatments may give rise to fewer ethical issues than treatments based on the physiological approach because…

Topic 3 Alternative therapies

You have to be able to discuss one alternative treatment to biological and behavioural therapies. You can choose either psychodynamic or cognitive–behavioural therapies (CBTs). In this workbook the focus is on CBTs. These therapies are based on the theory that how we feel is based on how we 'think' (cognition) and that 'faulty or irrational thinking' is the main cause of mental illness. For example, people suffering from depression may blame themselves unnecessarily for things that have gone wrong in their lives. Treatment, known as cognitive restructuring, aims to train people to think differently and, by doing this, to change their behaviour. The two most important types of CBT are rational emotive therapy and stress-inoculation therapy.

Item 1
Rational emotive therapy

Ellis (1957) developed rational emotive therapy (RET) based on the idea that some people have persistent self-defeating thoughts that are irrational. According to Ellis, irrational beliefs that may cause needless upset can be identified when we catch ourselves thinking 'should' or 'must' in ways that are subjective and judgemental. Thoughts such as 'I *must* be approved of by everybody' or 'I *should* always achieve in everything I do' are irrational. Believing these, or similar, irrational statements is self-defeating because this way of thinking prevents us from taking constructive action to change either ourselves or the situation. RET aims to challenge this way of thinking by helping clients to recognise their irrationality and the consequences of their habitual way of thinking. In RET, clients are taught to recognise and replace their 'irrational' thoughts with more constructive, realistic ones. As with behaviour modification, an ABC model can be used to explain what happens in RET:

- **A** — we experience an **activating event** leading to emotional arousal (e.g. receiving a poor grade in an exam).
- **B** — a **belief** is developed about the event that may be rational (e.g. I would have done better had I revised more effectively) or irrational (e.g. I must be thick and don't deserve to do better).
- **C** — behavioural **consequences** ensue from our beliefs which may be productive (e.g. deciding to resit the exam and revising fully) or unproductive (e.g. dropping out of class).

In RET, people are encouraged to realise that it is not the 'events in themselves' that lead to negative consequences but the self-defeating beliefs developed about the events. Clients are encouraged to change the way they think about events in their lives by internal disputation (arguing with themselves):

- **Logical disputation** — asking themselves whether the way they think 'makes sense'.
- **Empirical disputation** — asking themselves whether there is proof that their beliefs are accurate.
- **Pragmatic disputation** — asking themselves whether the way they think is helpful.

Effective internal disputation changes self-defeating beliefs into more rational beliefs that help clients feel better about themselves.

Item 2
Effectiveness, appropriateness and ethics of RET

Effectiveness
RET seems to be successful in treating some types of social anxiety. Research suggests that it can be used for the management of anger and depression and possibly stress.

Smith and Glass (1977) conducted a meta-analysis of therapies and cited RET as the second most effective of ten types of psychotherapy, the most effective being the behavioural therapy of systematic desensitisation. **Macaskill and Macaskill (1996)** reported that a combination of RET and drug therapy was more effective than medication alone.

RET for adult survivors of childhood sexual abuse
Möller and Steel (2002) assessed 26 adult survivors of childhood sexual abuse for depression, anxiety, anger, guilt and self-esteem before and after ten weekly sessions of group RET and at follow-up 8 weeks later. Cognitive restructuring was found to be effective in facilitating recovery from anxiety, depression and anger but less effective for guilt and low self-esteem. Only three patients recovered on all five variables; ten patients showed recovery on at least four variables. Relationship with the perpetrator and pre-treatment irrational evaluative beliefs (measured by means of the Survey of Personal Beliefs) were found to be the best predictors of treatment outcome.

Recovery was more likely if the perpetrator of the abuse was a stranger rather than a close family member. Also, there was a negative correlation between the rate of self-directed 'shoulds' and negative self-worth beliefs.

Appropriateness
There are some problems with evaluating the appropriateness of RET. First, it is difficult to define 'irrational thinking', and psychologists cannot agree on this. RET therapists and their clients have to decide and agree which thought patterns should be changed. Second, RET may only be effective with a biased sample of the population — those who have insight into their condition, who are articulate and who have the time and money for such treatment. This limits the generalisability of RET. The term YAVIS has been used to describe this biased sample of clients – **y**oung, **a**ttractive, **v**erbal, **i**ntelligent and **s**uccessful.

Is RET ethical?
The 'judgemental' aspect of RET, in which clients are 'persuaded' that their thought patterns may be irrational, may present ethical concerns. **Alloy and Abrahmson (1979)** found that depressed people gave more accurate estimates of the probability of disaster than non-depressed people. Optimistic beliefs may be just as 'irrational' as the pessimistic ones held by depressives, but they are less self-defeating. Perhaps, rather than pessimistic thought patterns being described as irrational, they should be described as unhealthy.

Item 3
Stress-inoculation therapy

Meichenbaum (1985) developed stress-inoculation therapy (SIT). Like RET, this therapy aims to teach clients to replace self-defeating thoughts with more positive ones and to practise this until it becomes a habit.

SIT is a way of training people to be able to cope with stress before it becomes a serious problem. It can be used in many workplace situations to help people manage their jobs better. Unlike other therapies, SIT is a *preventative* treatment for stress-related mental disorders that have seriously damaging effects on people's lives.

Meichenbaum proposed that SIT could prepare people to cope with stress in the same way that an injection prevents a disease. There are three stages in SIT:
- **Conceptualisation.** Clients identify and express their feelings and fears and are encouraged to relive stressful situations, analysing what was stressful about them and how they attempted to deal with them.
- **Skill acquisition and rehearsal.** Clients learn how to relax and perhaps to turn to others for support. Specific skills such as parenting techniques, communication skills, time management or study skills may be taught.
- **Application and follow through.** The therapist guides patients through progressively more threatening situations so that they can apply their newly acquired skills. The techniques become reinforced and this makes the practices self-sustaining.

Item 4
Effectiveness and appropriateness of SIT

Effectiveness
Stress inoculation has been effective in a variety of stressful situations, ranging from anxiety about mathematics in college students, managing hypertension in all age groups and stress management in general. It has been successfully combined with other treatment methods to alleviate stress.

Stress inoculation to help people control anger
Raymond Novaco (1995) demonstrated the usefulness of stress-inoculation training and relaxation in helping people to control anger. He trained patients who were both self-identified and clinically assessed as having serious problems in controlling anger. Participants learnt about the role of arousal and cognitive processes in feelings of anger. They then learned to relax their muscles while making 'self-statements' (telling themselves) such as those in Table 1.

The participants practised the techniques while imagining and role-playing realistic anger situations that were arranged in a hierarchy from least to most provoking. As measured by self-reports and their blood pressure, when provoked in the therapeutic situation they were able to control their anger.

Peer-led SIT
Fontana et al. (1999) studied the effectiveness of peer-led SIT in college students. After a six-session treatment programme

Table 1 *Self-statements*

Situation	Self-statements
Preparing for a provocation	This could be a tough situation but I know how to deal with it. I can work out a plan to handle this. Remember not to take it personally.
Impact and confrontation	As long as I keep my cool then I am in control of the situation. I don't need to prove myself. There is no point in getting mad. Look for the positives and don't jump to conclusions.
Coping with arousal	Muscles are getting tight so relax and slow things down. Time to take a deep breath. My anger is a signal of what I need to do.
Subsequent reflection if conflict was unresolved	Forget about the aggravation. Thinking about it only makes you upset. Try to shake it off. Don't take it personally.
Subsequent reflection if conflict was resolved	I handled that one pretty well. That's doing a good job. I could have got more upset than it was worth. I'm doing better at this all the time. I got through that without getting angry.

participants had lower heart rates and anxiety levels than controls. This difference was shown to have been maintained at a 6-month follow-up.

Appropriateness

SIT focuses on both the nature of the stress problem (enabling clients to appraise their life more realistically) and on ways of coping with stress, which gives clients greater understanding of the strengths and limitations of specific techniques. Also, SIT has a wide range of applications, from dealing with chronic stressors such as chronic pain, to dealing with the effects of divorce or bereavement. The focus on skills acquisition means that the benefits of SIT may be long-lasting. However, a programme of treatment is complex and takes a long time, and as with RET, SIT may only be effective with a biased (YAVIS) sample of the ppopulation. This limits its generalisability. There may be fewer ethical problems with SIT than with RET, because SIT is non-judgemental. Rather than being told that their thinking is irrational, clients identify problem areas to be worked on.

Item 5
Combining cognitive behavioural therapies

Roskies (1986) randomly assigned men who exhibited the type–A behaviour pattern (competitive, time-pressured and stressed) to either a multimodal therapy programme or to one of two physical exercise groups (aerobic training or weight training). The multimodal therapy included progressive muscle relaxation and most aspects of RET and SIT. It was used to control:
- physical tension through relaxation
- emotional outbursts through RET
- interpersonal friction through SIT

All participants attended two or three sessions a week for 10 weeks. The men were interviewed at the end of the training period and their blood pressure and heart rate were assessed in response to stressors (e.g. doing mental arithmetic). None of the three treatments reduced the men's physiological reactivity, but the multimodal programme was more successful in reducing some aspects of type-A behaviour, such as competitiveness and hostility.

A2 Psychology: Treating Mental Disorders

1 Read your textbook and Items 1–3.
   a Fill in the blanks to complete the sentences.

Topic 3 Alternative therapies

Answers

1a (i) Cognitive–behavioural therapies are based on the theory that .... thinking is the main cause of mental illness.

(ii) Irrational beliefs can be identified when we catch ourselves thinking .... or .... in ways that are subjective and self-judgemental.

(iii) RET stands for ....

(iv) In RET, clients are encouraged to change the way they think about their experiences by ....

(v) .... disputation is when clients ask themselves whether the way they think 'makes sense'.

(vi) Empirical disputation is when clients ask themselves whether there is .... that their beliefs are accurate.

(vii) Pragmatic disputation is when clients ask themselves whether the way they think is .... to them.

(viii) Effective internal disputation changes self-defeating beliefs into more .... beliefs.

(ix) SIT stands for ....

(x) SIT is a .... treatment for stress-related mental disorders.

b Outline the aim of cognitive–behavioural therapy (CBT).

b ....

c Ellis (1957) believed that some people can 'talk themselves' into having psychological problems such as depression. Explain Ellis's theory.

c

d Outline the ABC of irrational thinking.

d

e Outline how rational emotive therapy (RET) can help people.

e

A2 Psychology: Treating Mental Disorders

Topic 3 Alternative therapies

f Even though Tara has revised hard, she 'knows' she will fail her final exams. She lies awake every night thinking how awful it will be to be left behind when all her friends go to university. In terms of RET, suggest how Tara could be helped to overcome her needless anxiety.

f

2 Read your textbook and Item 2. Based on psychological evidence, write two paragraphs (each continuing the 'starter statement') to suggest whether RET is effective and appropriate as a treatment for some mental disorders.

2a There is evidence to suggest that RET is effective…

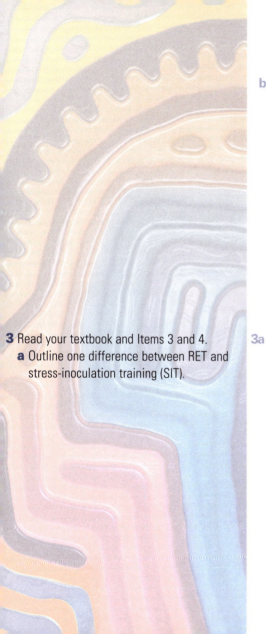

b However, RET may not always be an appropriate treatment…

3 Read your textbook and Items 3 and 4.
  a Outline one difference between RET and stress-inoculation training (SIT).

3a

A2 Psychology: Treating Mental Disorders

Topic 3 Alternative therapies

b Identify the three stages in SIT.

c Jonah is expected to give a speech at a dinner for many invited guests. However, he hates public speaking and because he is terrified of making a fool of himself he is anxious and stressed. Mr Meichenbaum has offered to help Jonah overcome his fear of public speaking. Write a letter to Jonah explaining what will happen during SIT.

d Outline evidence that suggests that SIT treatment is effective.

d

4 Read your textbook and Items 1–5.
  a Outline one reason why the effects of SIT may be more long-lasting than the effects of RET.

4a

A2 Psychology: Treating Mental Disorders

Topic 3 Alternative therapies

b Outline one reason why SIT may be more ethically appropriate than RET.

b

5 Read your textbook and review all the items in Topics 1, 2 and 3.

Cassandra has been diagnosed as suffering from depression, and she believes that nothing good will ever happen to her. She has been offered drug therapy or RET but cannot decide which of these treatments might be best for her.

Based on what you have learned about these treatments, write a letter to Cassandra discussing the appropriateness and effectiveness of each of these two types of treatment. You should write about 400 words.

5

(cont. overleaf)

A2 Psychology: Treating Mental Disorders

Topic 3 Alternative therapies